MW00366445

WHY TRUDEAU IS A GREAT LEADER

& DESERVES RESPECT

HENRY MAPLE PHD

WHY TRUDEAU IS A GREAT LEADER

.

WHY TRUDEAU IS A GREAT LEADER

WHY TRUDEAU IS A GREAT LEADER

WHY TRUDEAU IS A GREAT LEADER

WHY TRUDEAU IS A GREAT LEADER

WHY TRUDEAU IS A GREAT LEADER

WHY TRUDEAU IS A GREAT LEADER

WHY TRUDEAU IS A GREAT LEADER

WHY TRUDEAU IS A GREAT LEADER

WHY TRUDEAU IS A GREAT LEADER

WHY TRUDEAU IS A GREAT LEADER

WHY TRUDEAU IS A GREAT LEADER

WHY TRUDEAU IS A GREAT LEADER

WHY TRUDEAU IS A GREAT LEADER

WHY TRUDEAU IS A GREAT LEADER

WHY TRUDEAU IS A GREAT LEADER

WHY TRUDEAU IS A GREAT LEADER

WHY TRUDEAU IS A GREAT LEADER

WHY TRUDEAU IS A GREAT LEADER

.

WHY TRUDEAU IS A GREAT LEADER

WHY TRUDEAU IS A GREAT LEADER

WHY TRUDEAU IS A GREAT LEADER

WHY TRUDEAU IS A GREAT LEADER

WHY TRUDEAU IS A GREAT LEADER

WHY TRUDEAU IS A GREAT LEADER

WHY TRUDEAU IS A GREAT LEADER

WHY TRUDEAU IS A GREAT LEADER

WHY TRUDEAU IS A GREAT LEADER

WHY TRUDEAU IS A GREAT LEADER

WHY TRUDEAU IS A GREAT LEADER

WHY TRUDEAU IS A GREAT LEADER

.

WHY TRUDEAU IS A GREAT LEADER

WHY TRUDEAU IS A GREAT LEADER

WHY TRUDEAU IS A GREAT LEADER

WHY TRUDEAU IS A GREAT LEADER

WHY TRUDEAU IS A GREAT LEADER

.

WHY TRUDEAU IS A GREAT LEADER

.

WHY TRUDEAU IS A GREAT LEADER

.

WHY TRUDEAU IS A GREAT LEADER

WHY TRUDEAU IS A GREAT LEADER

WHY TRUDEAU IS A GREAT LEADER

WHY TRUDEAU IS A GREAT LEADER

WHY TRUDEAU IS A GREAT LEADER

WHY TRUDEAU IS A GREAT LEADER

WHY TRUDEAU IS A GREAT LEADER

WHY TRUDEAU IS A GREAT LEADER

WHY TRUDEAU IS A GREAT LEADER

WHY TRUDEAU IS A GREAT LEADER

.

WHY TRUDEAU IS A GREAT LEADER

.

.

WHY TRUDEAU IS A GREAT LEADER

WHY TRUDEAU IS A GREAT LEADER

WHY TRUDEAU IS A GREAT LEADER